I0468894

Better Than Zen

Adult Coloring Book

Volume 1: Calming Kaleidoscopes

25 Meditative Coloring Patterns
Designed To Relax And Enlighten

www.AddictedToColoring.com

Copyright © 2015 Natalie James

Welcome To Better Than Zen
Adult Coloring Book Volume One

I have designed this adult coloring book with engaging and hypnotic pattern pages to capture your focus and relax your mind, helping create a "Zen like" state.

Sometimes life feels out of control. Calling a "time out" to focus on a single interesting task can be very helpful. This coloring book was created to allow you to do just that.

These 25 designs are each printed on a single page so you can use any of your coloring supplies to create your own stunning works of art.

I truly hope these coloring pages bring you hours of enjoyment.

Yours In Coloring,
Natalie James
AddictedToColoring.com

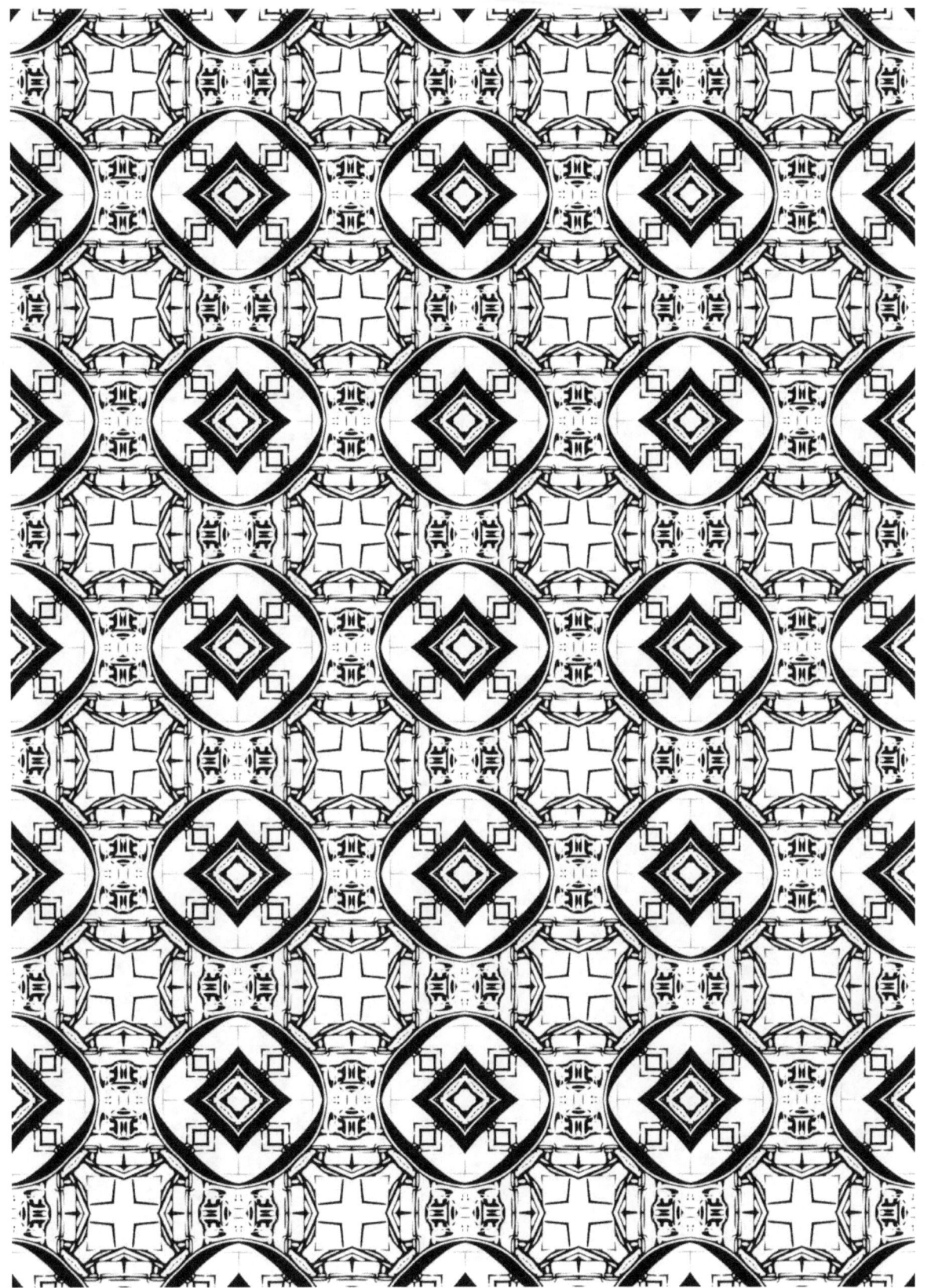

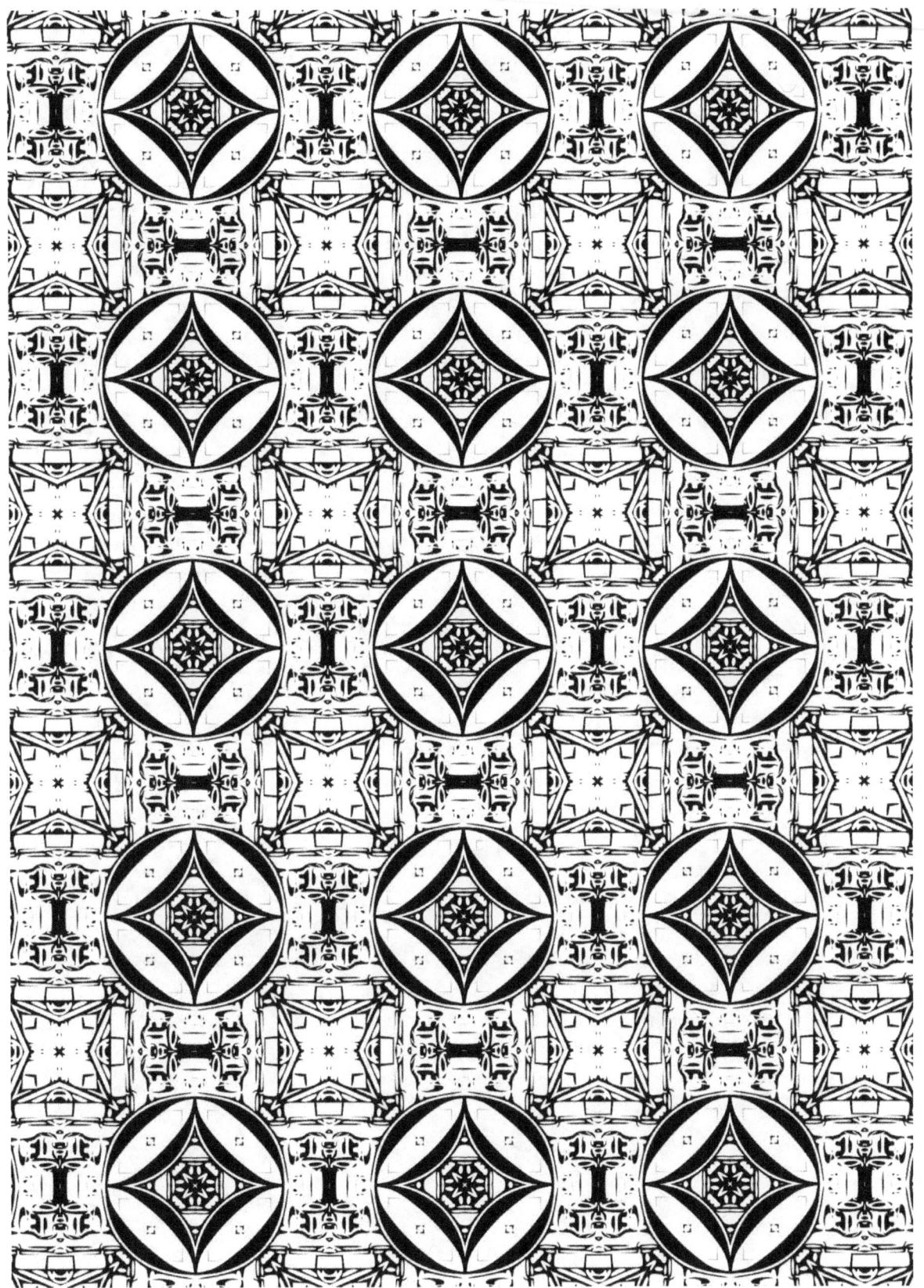

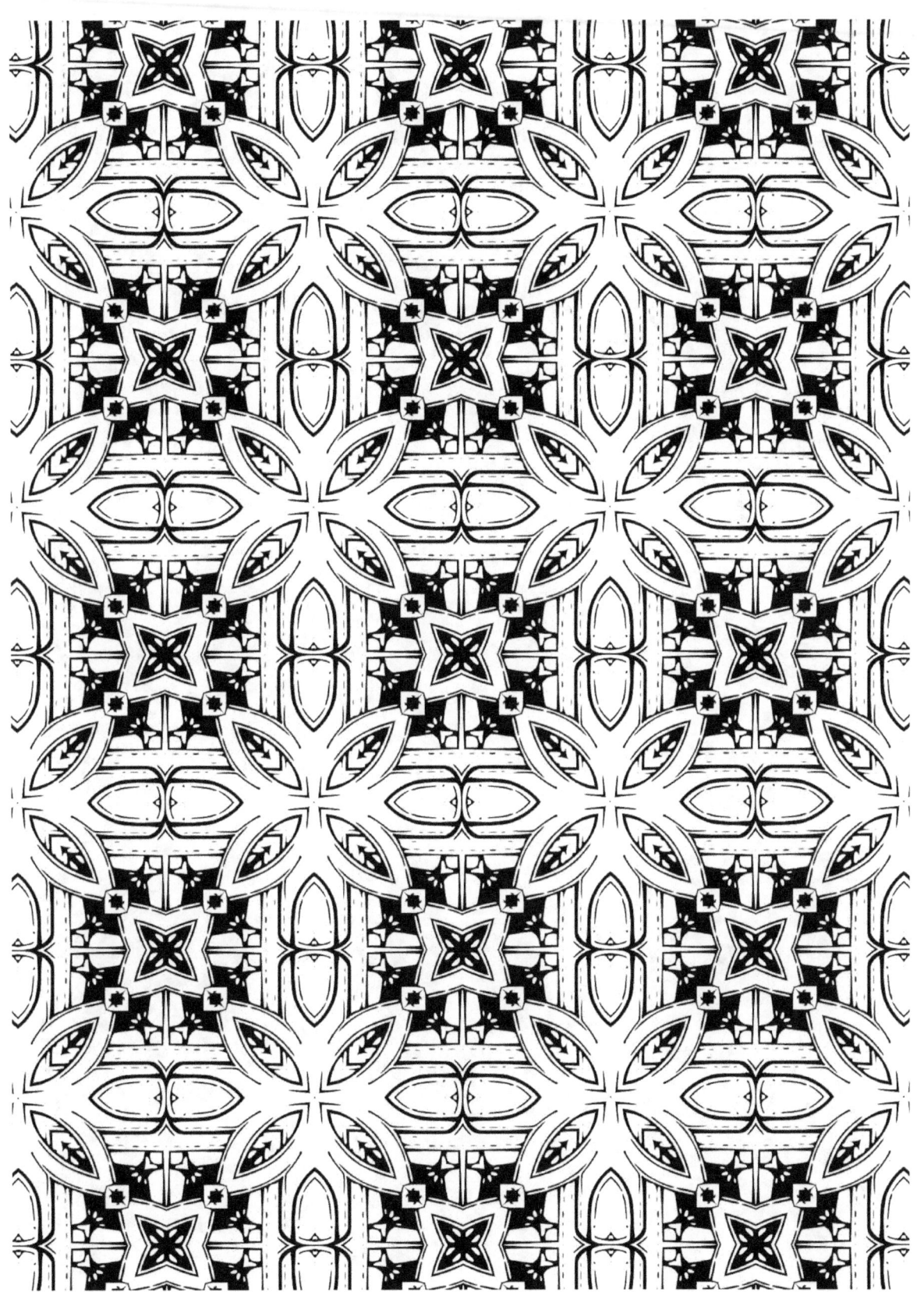

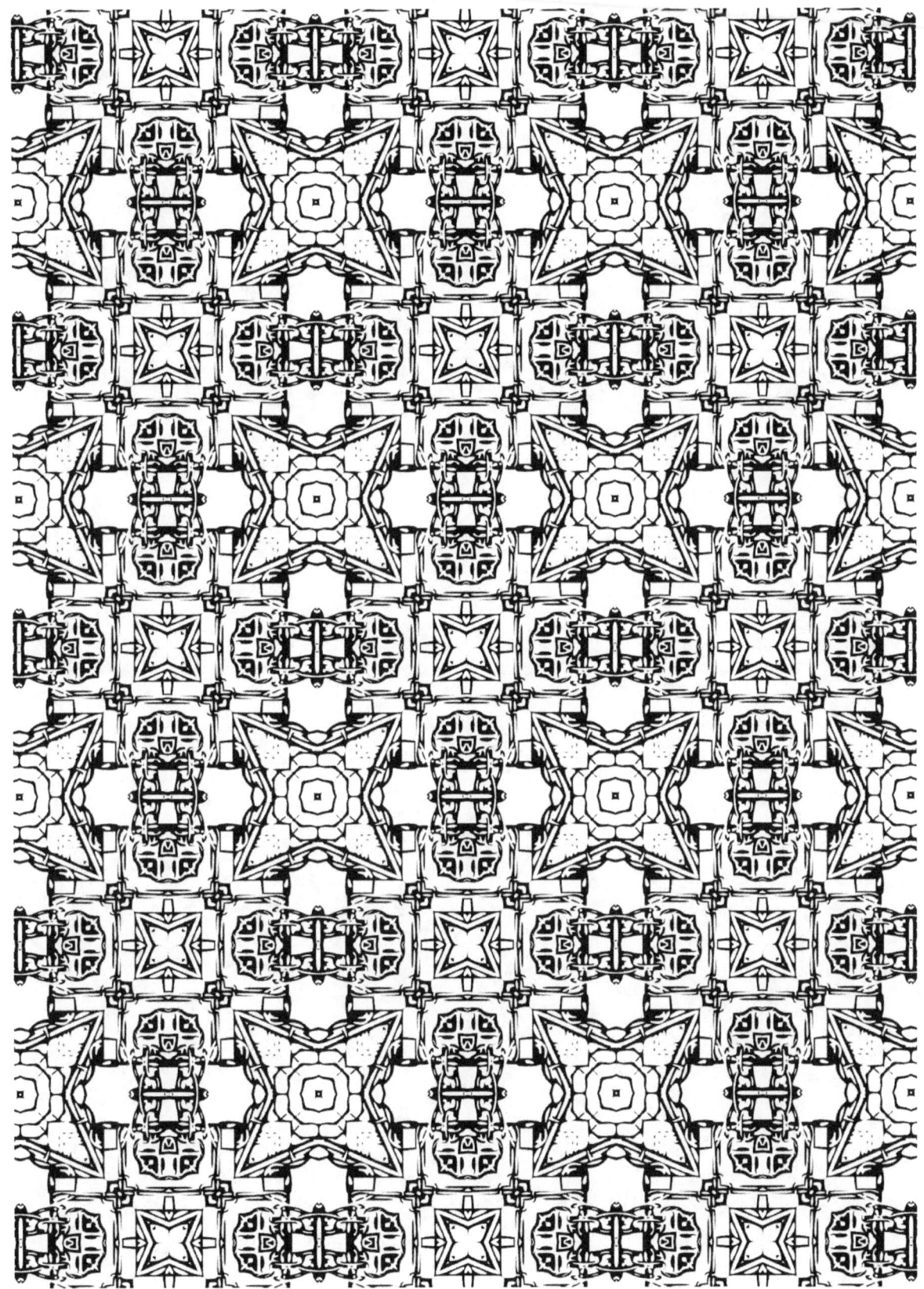

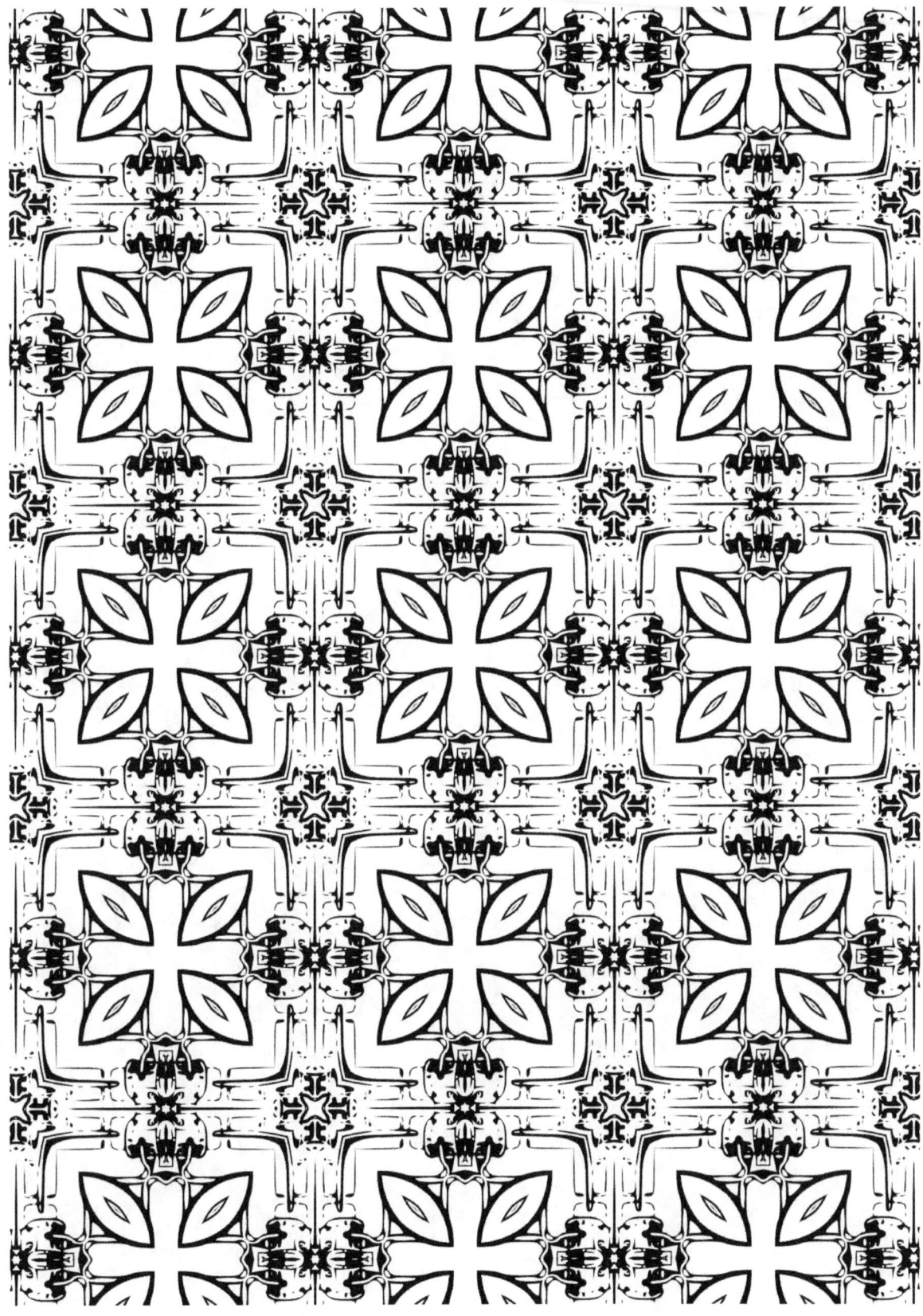

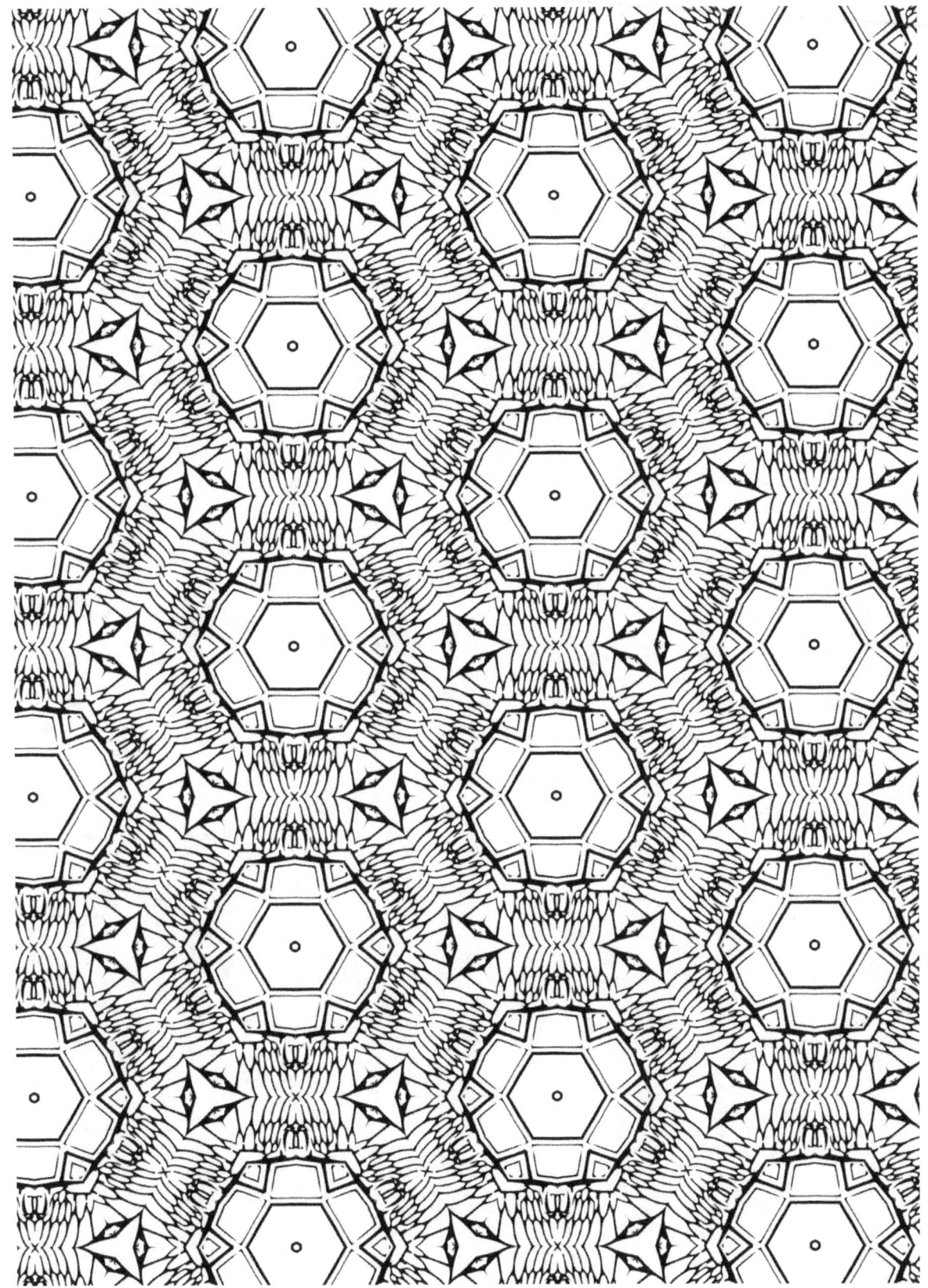

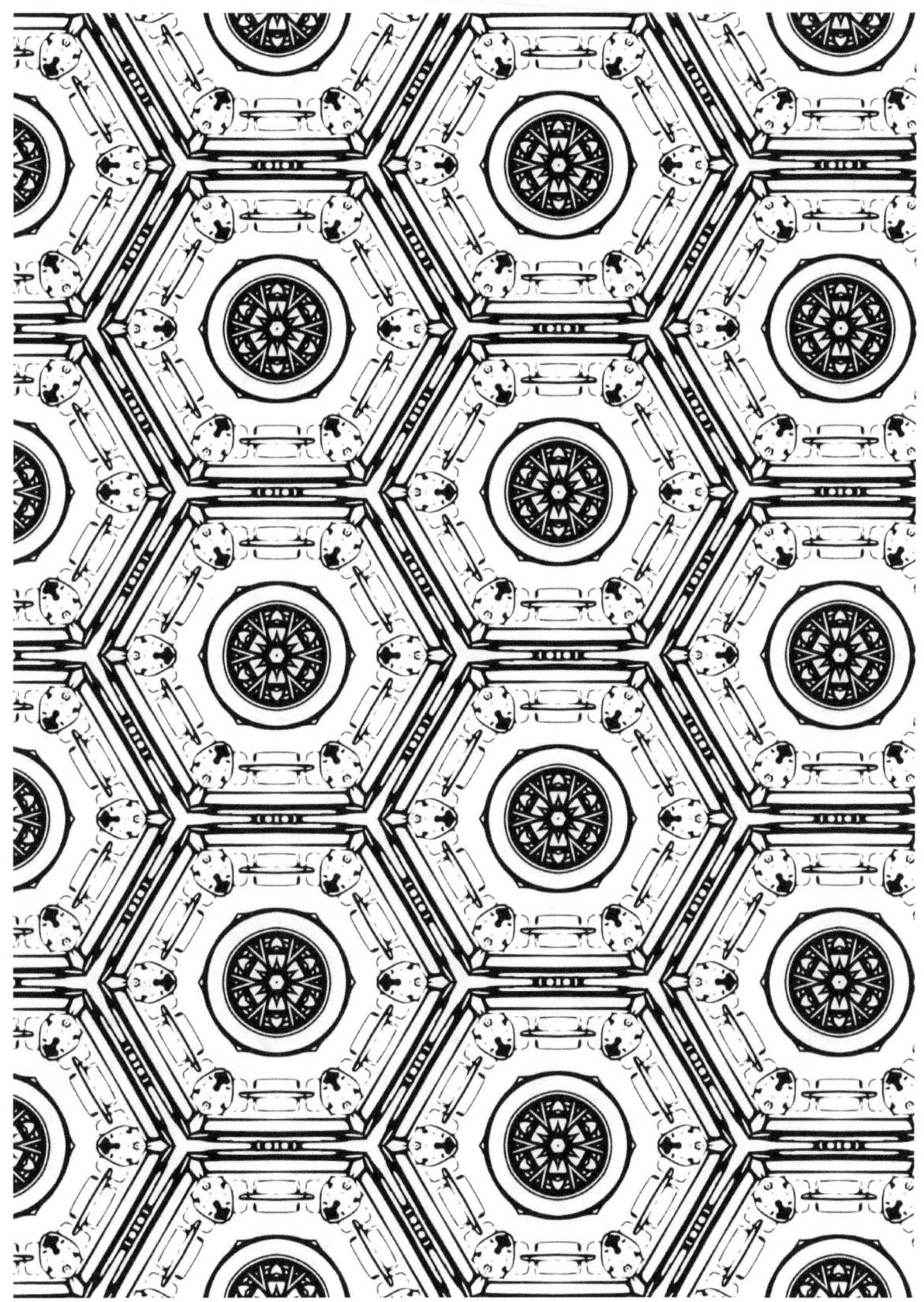

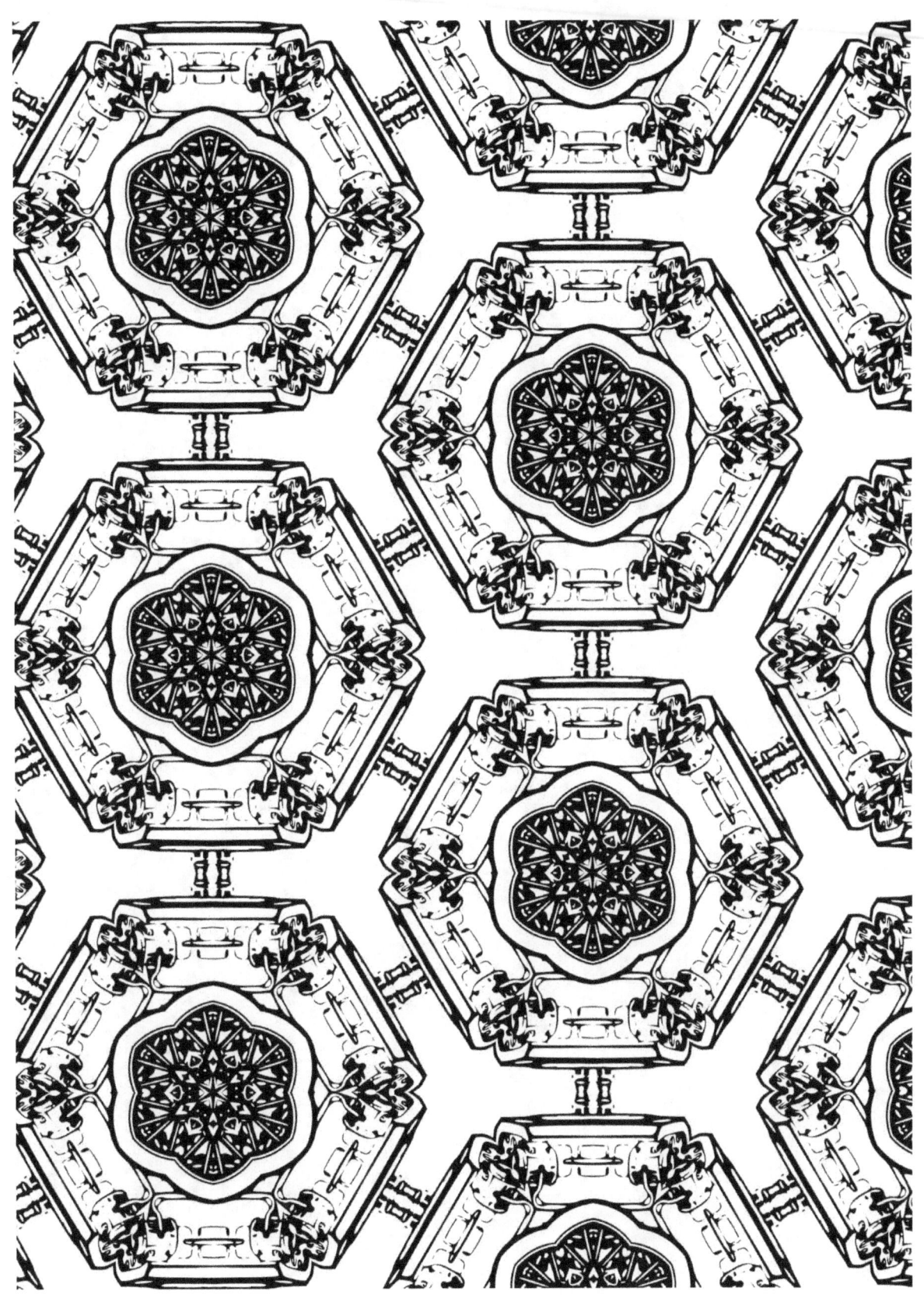

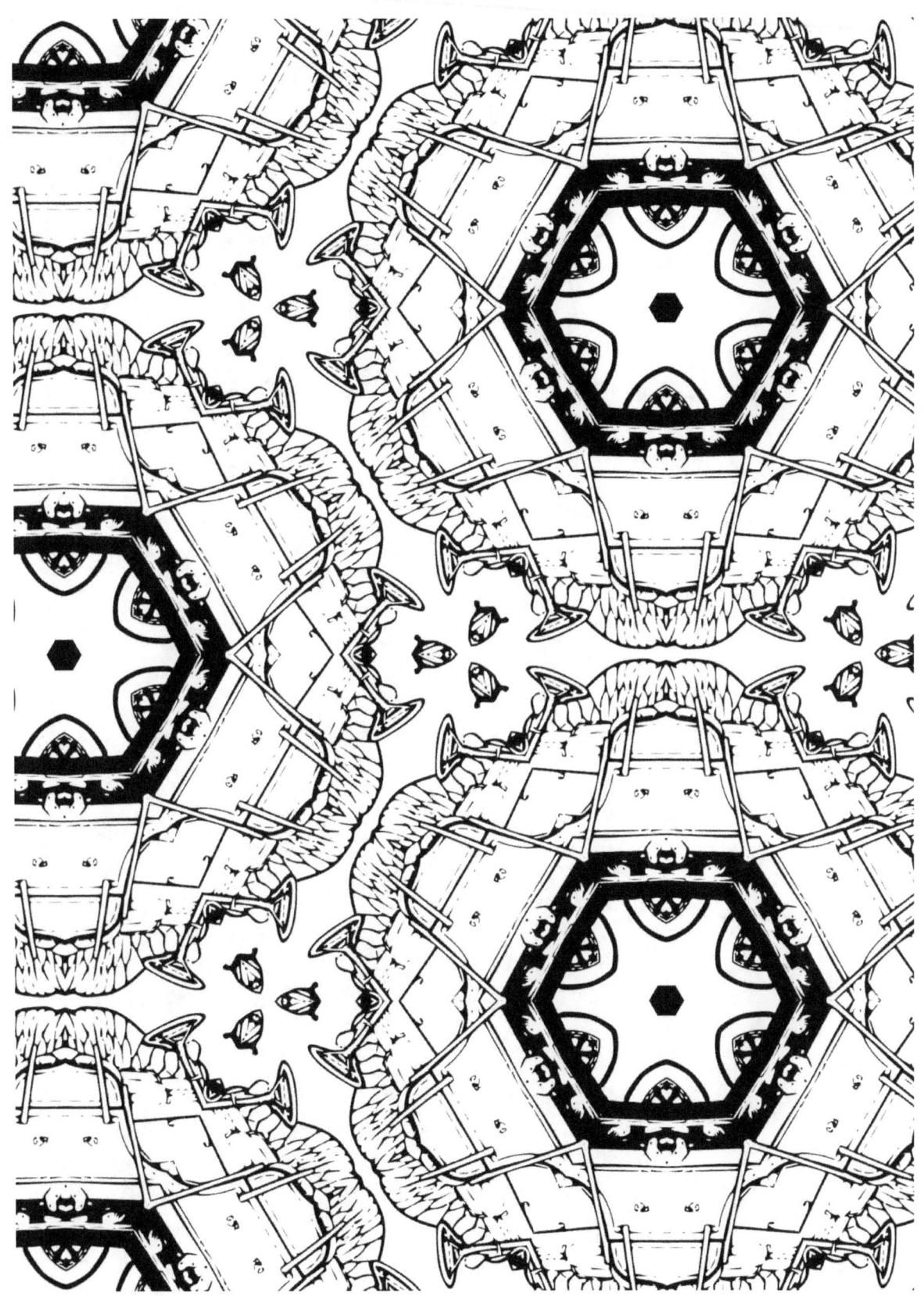

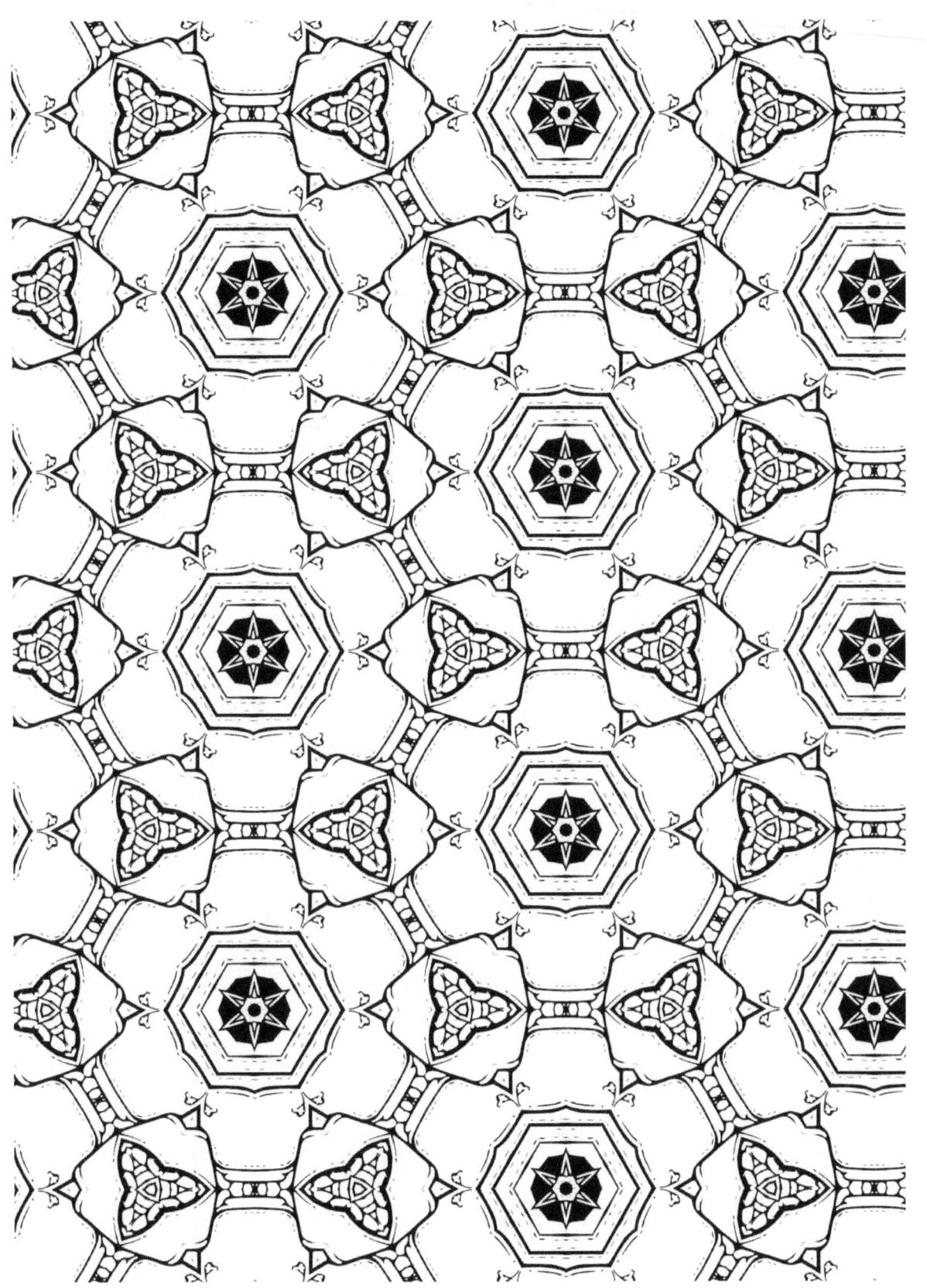

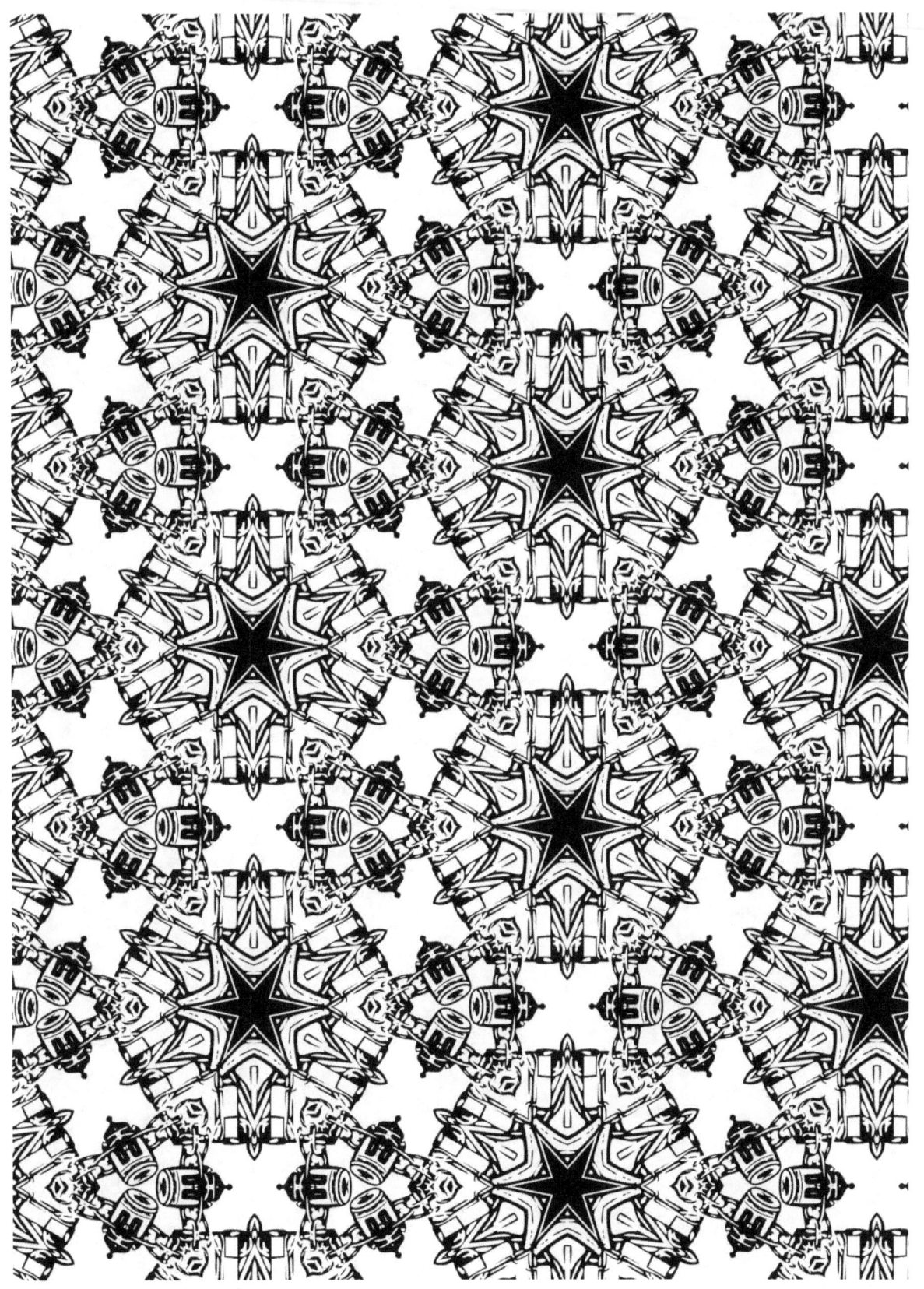

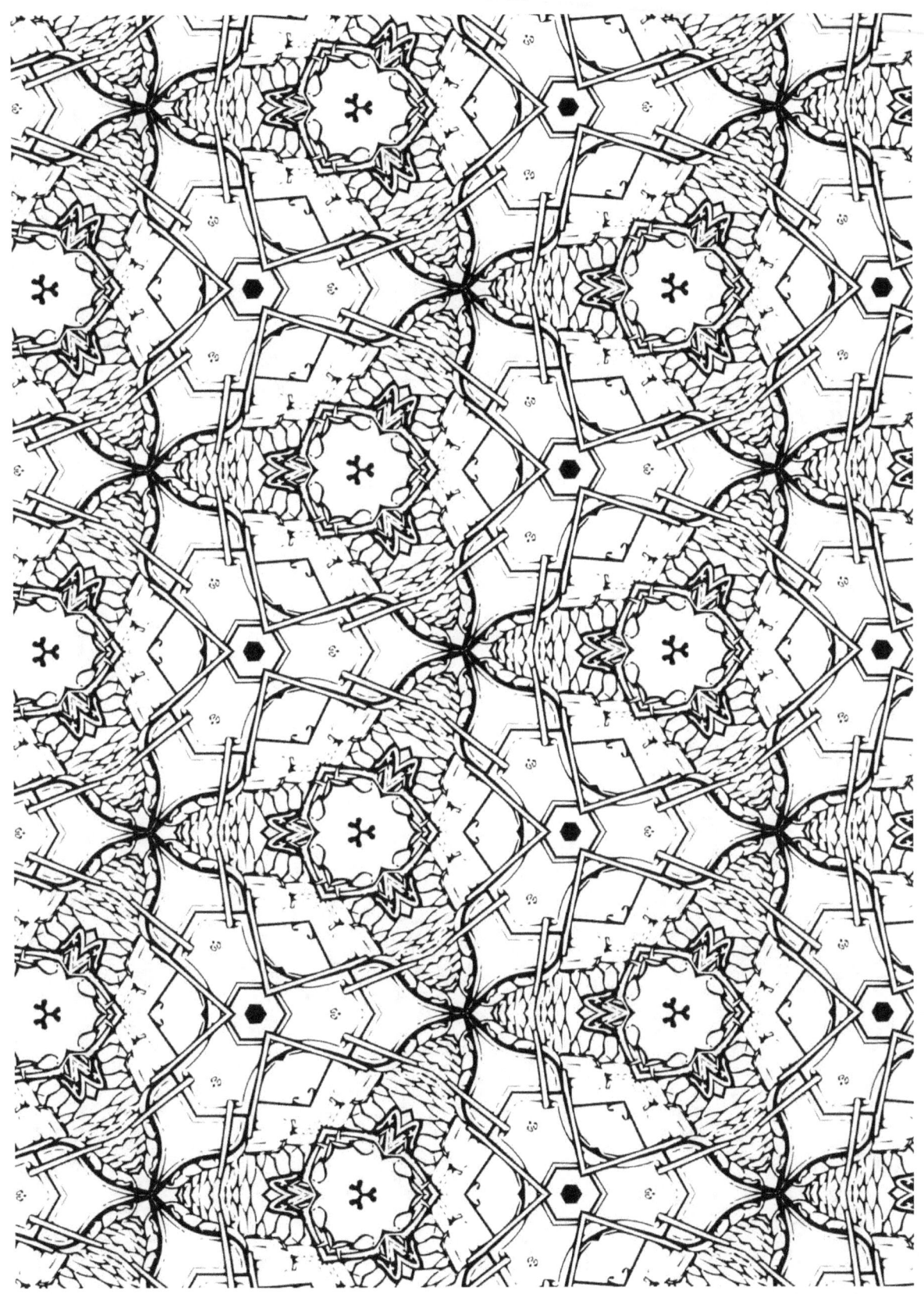

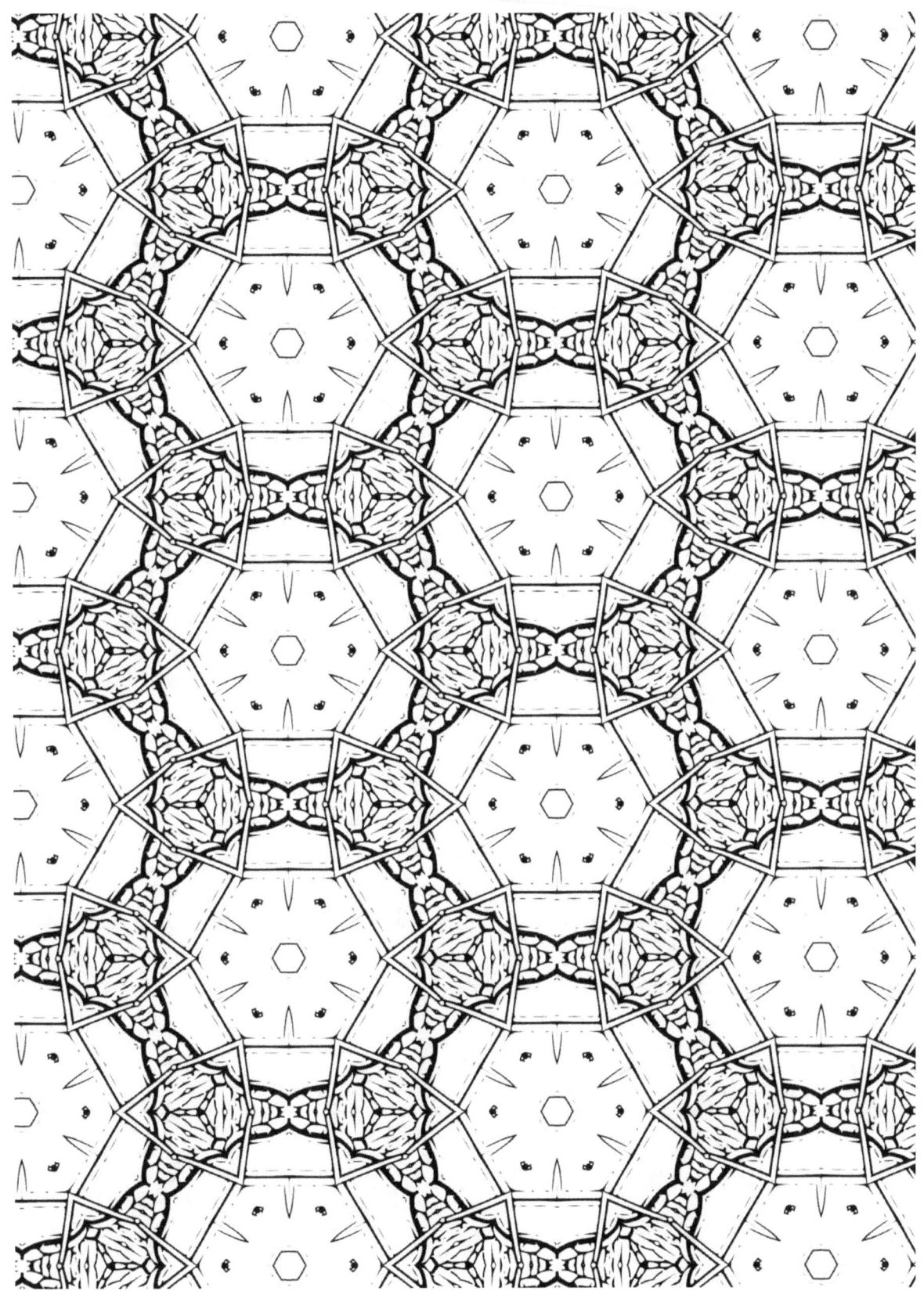

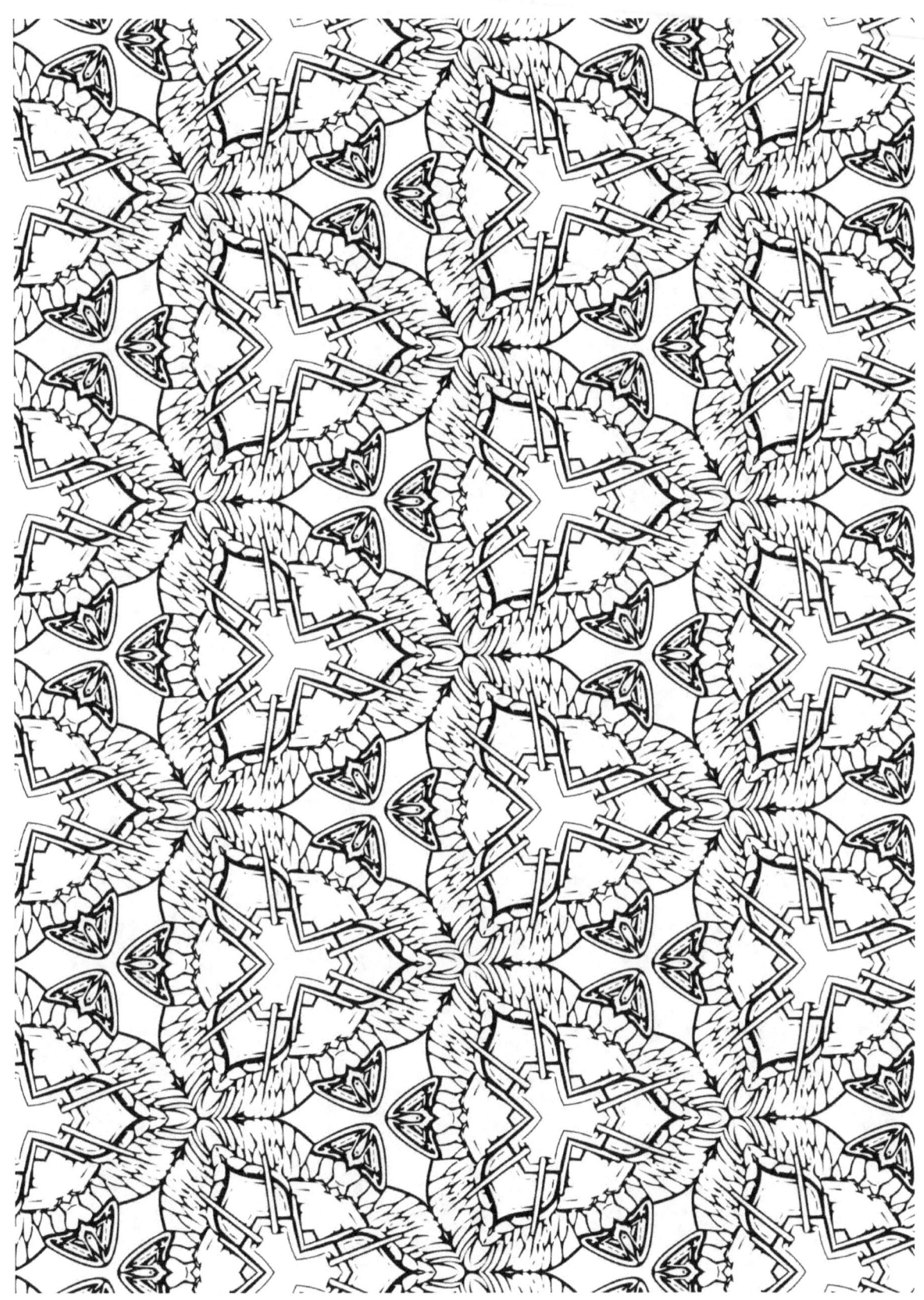

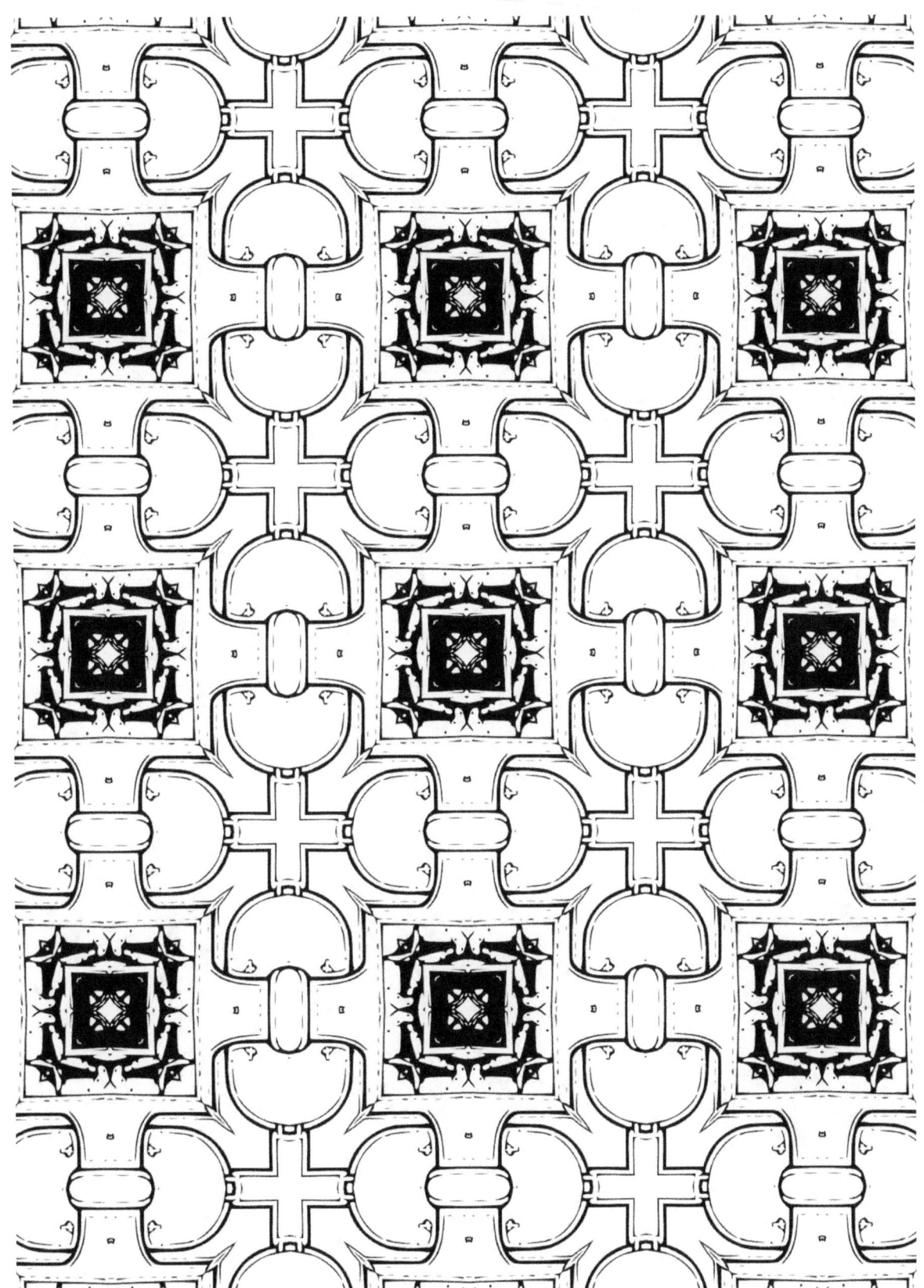

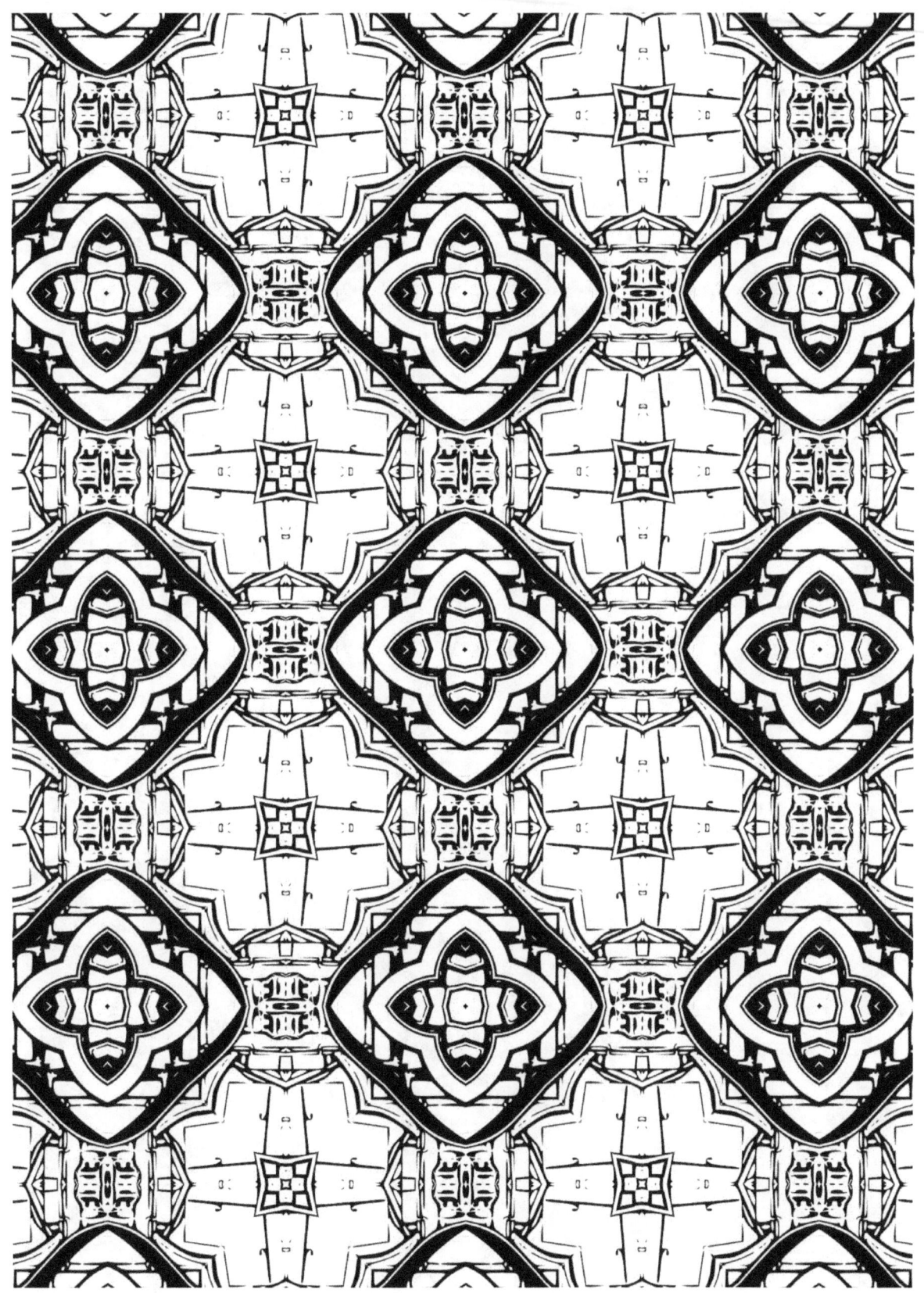

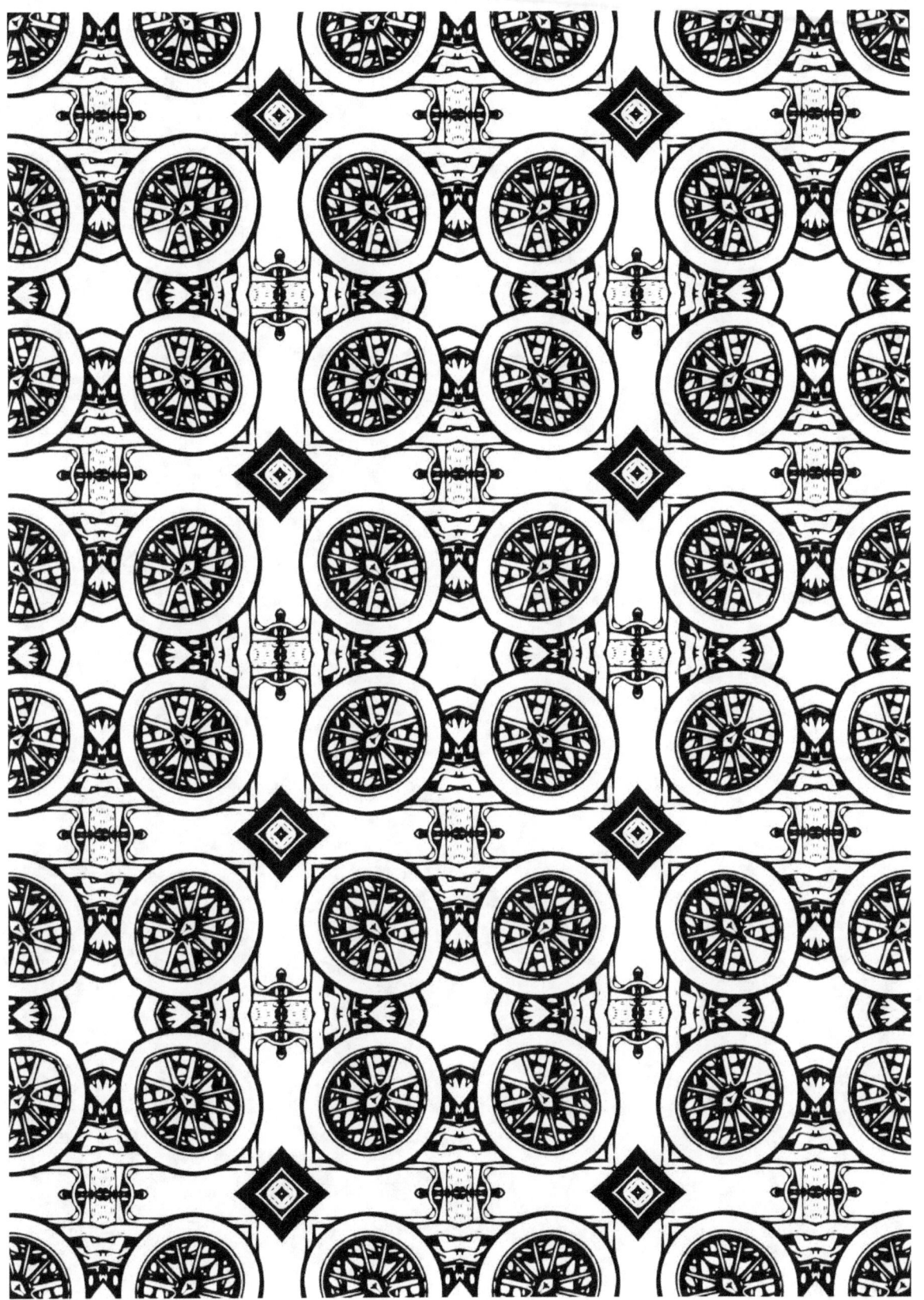

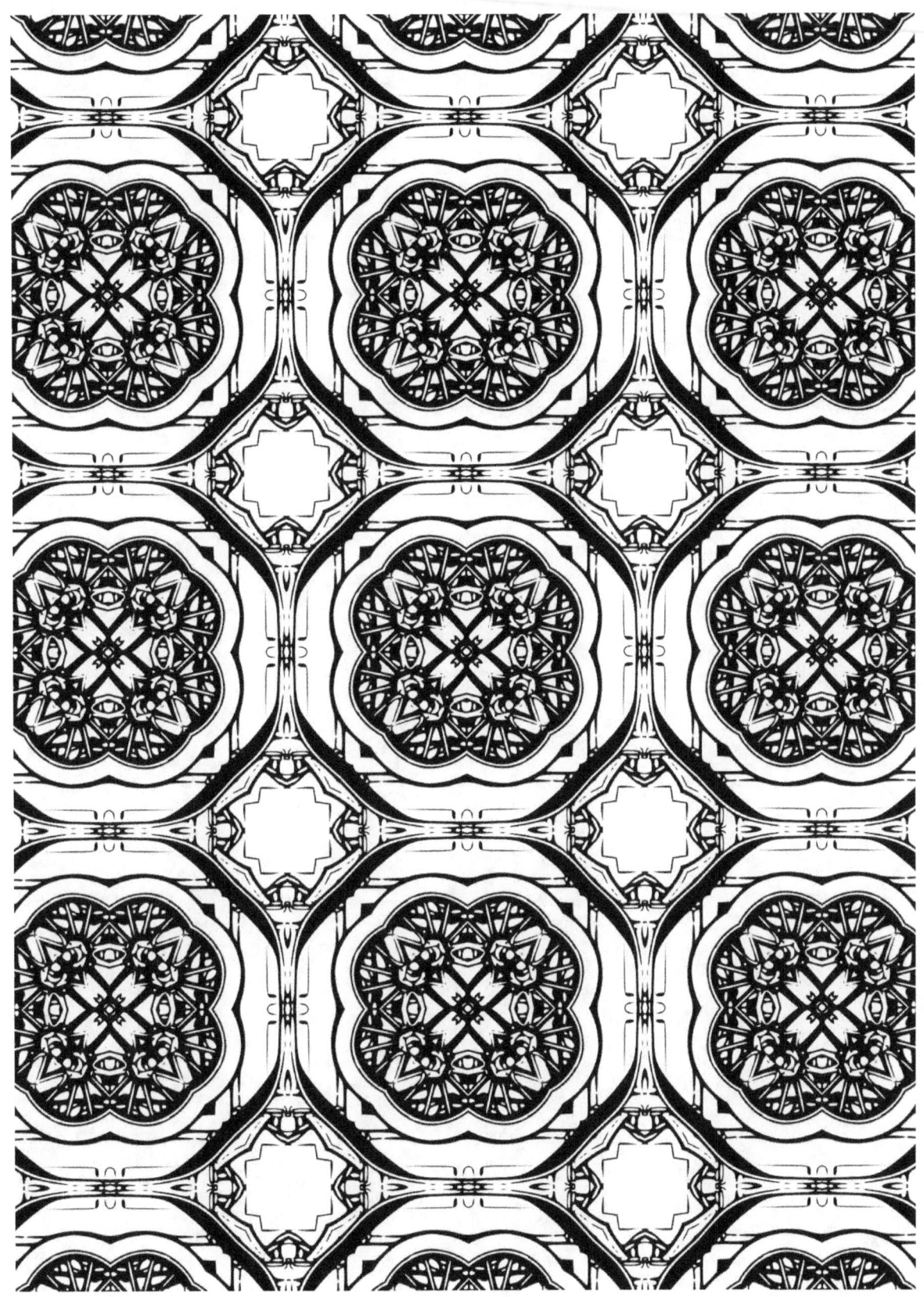

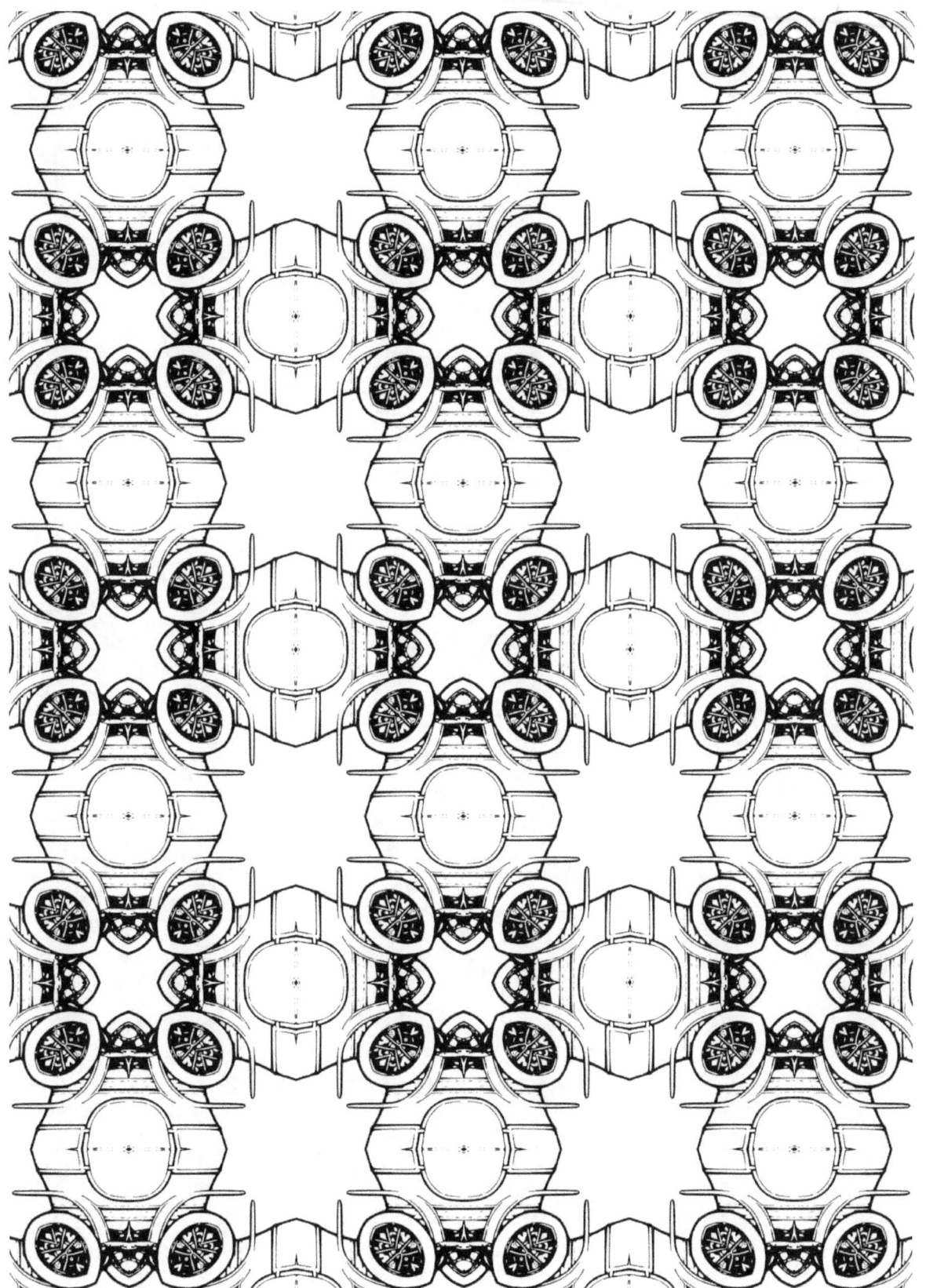

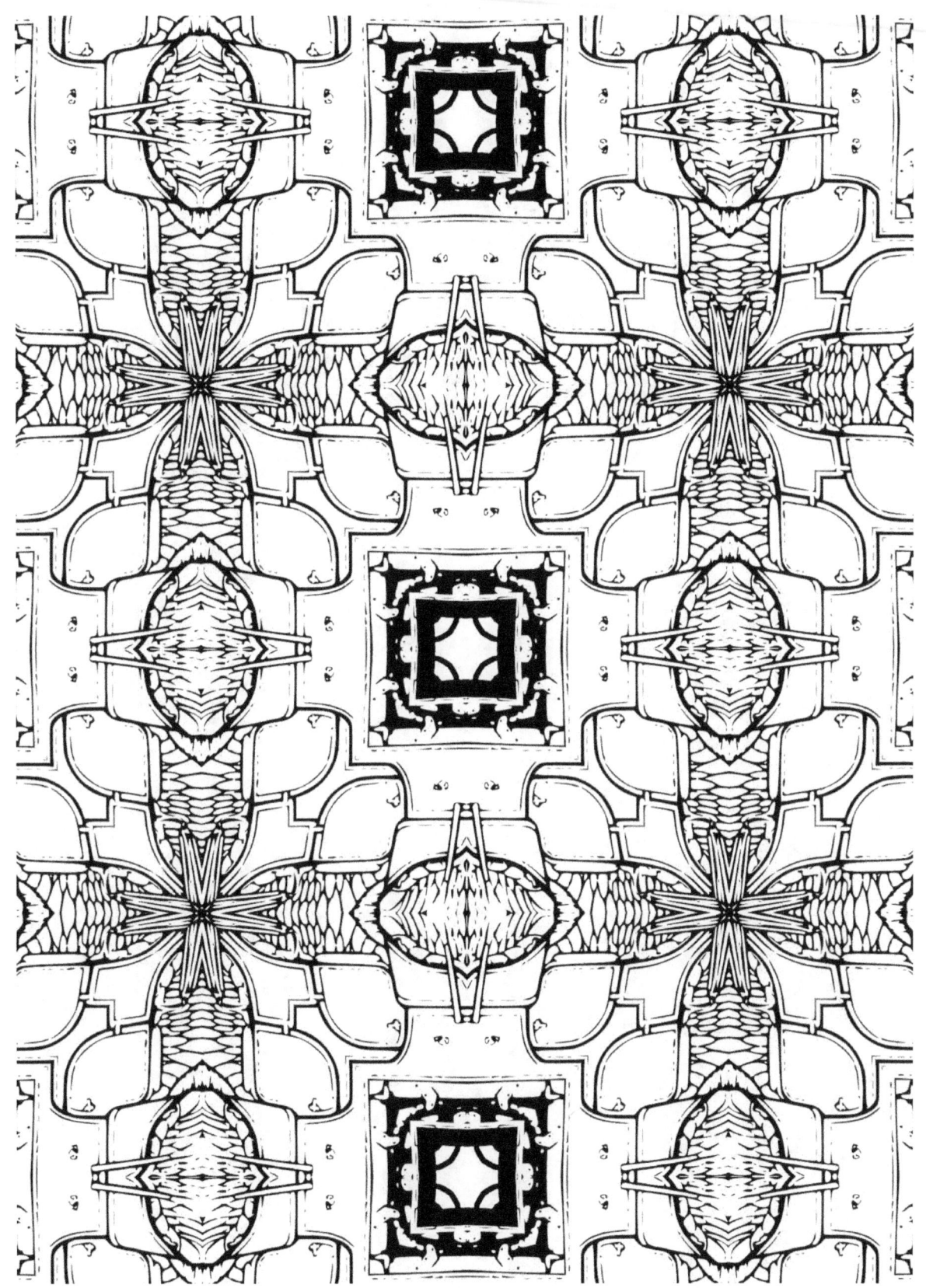

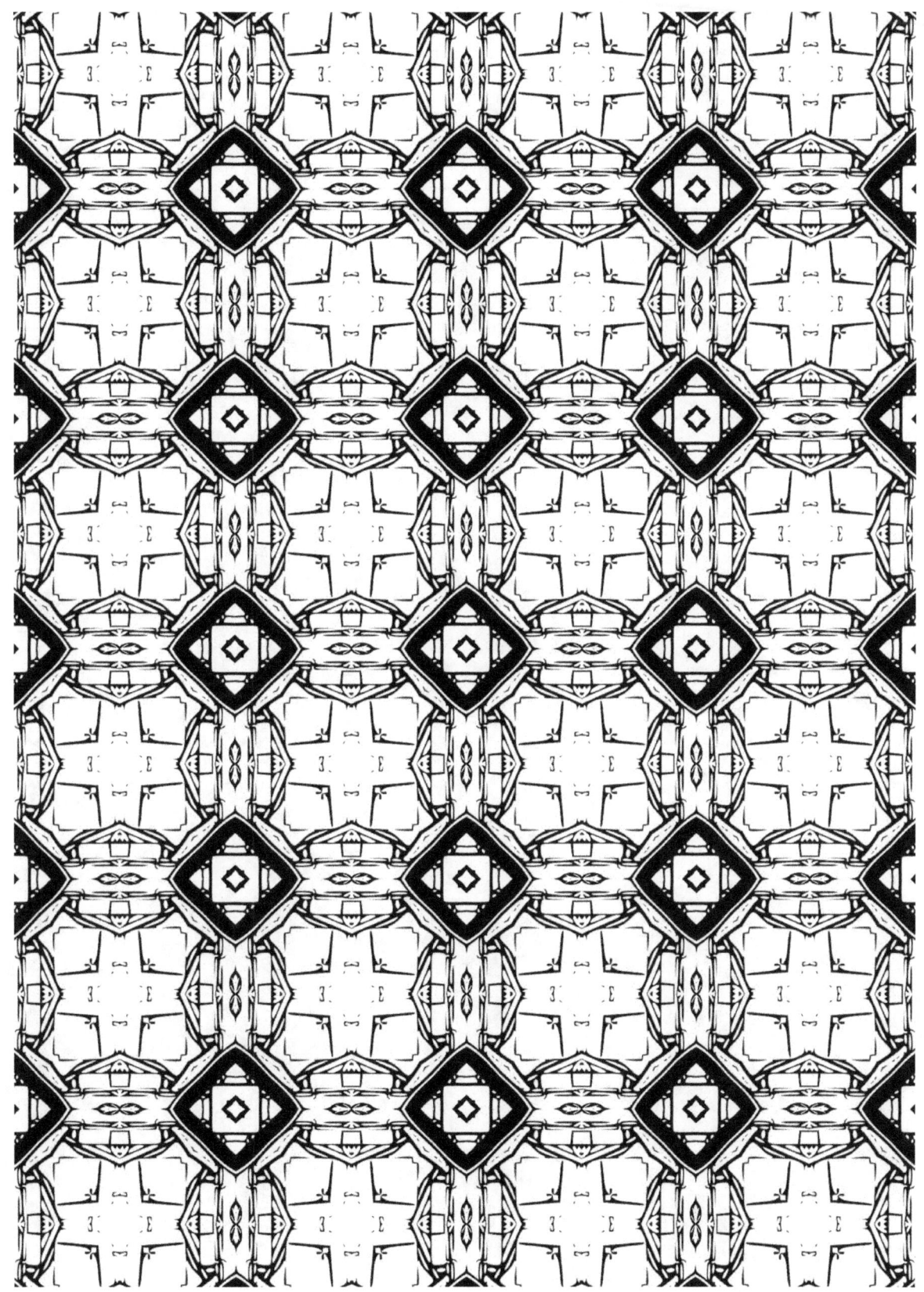

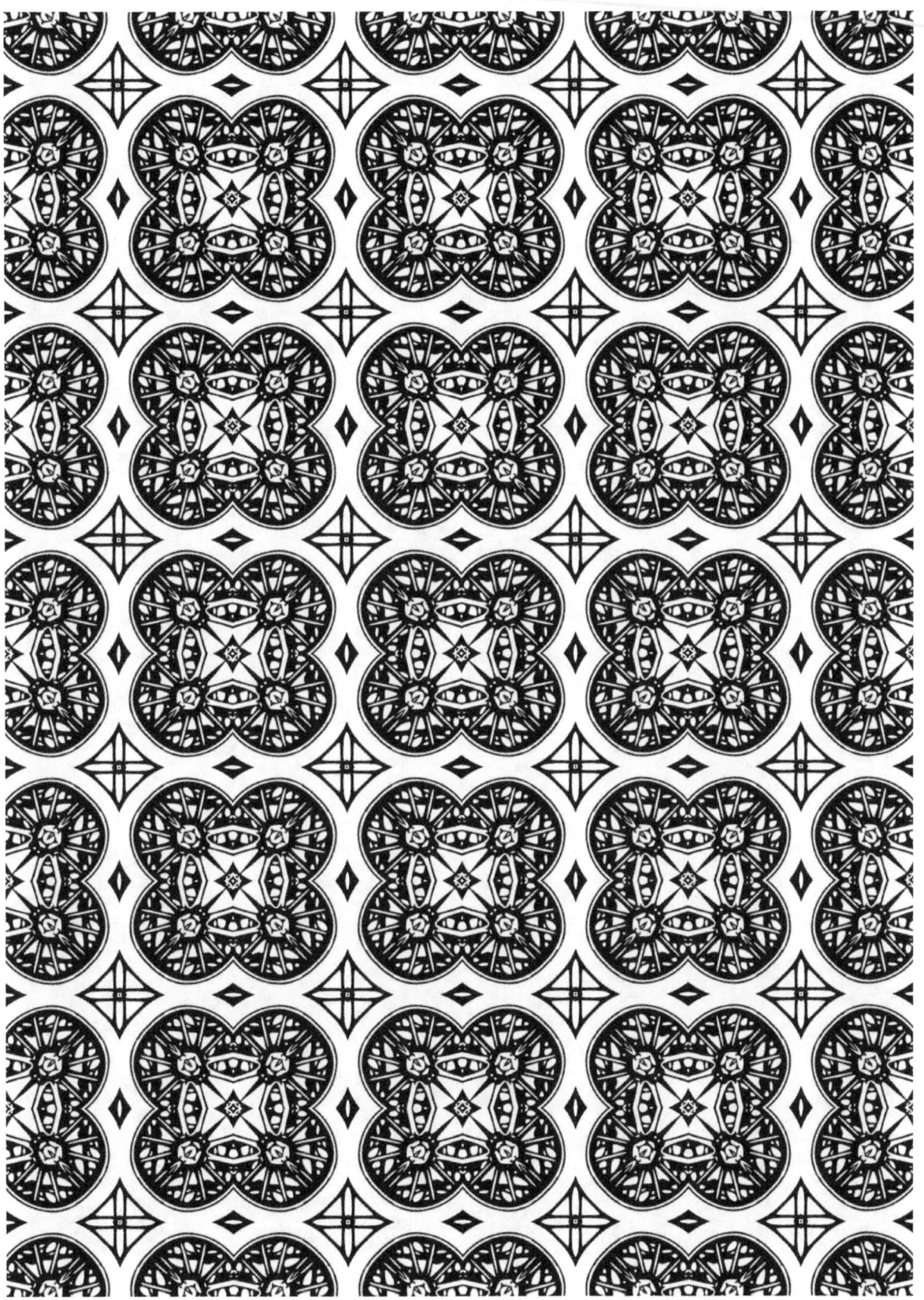

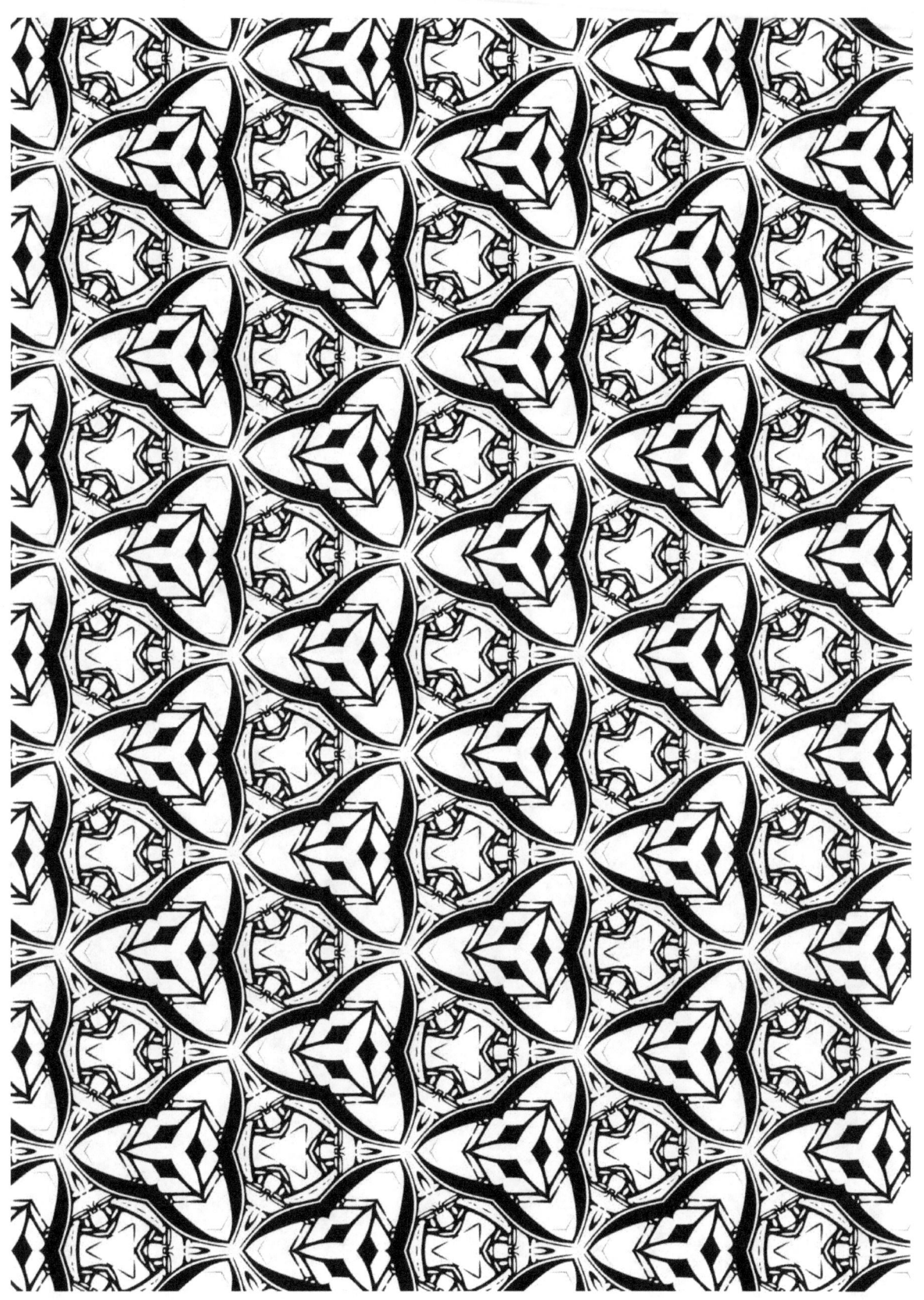

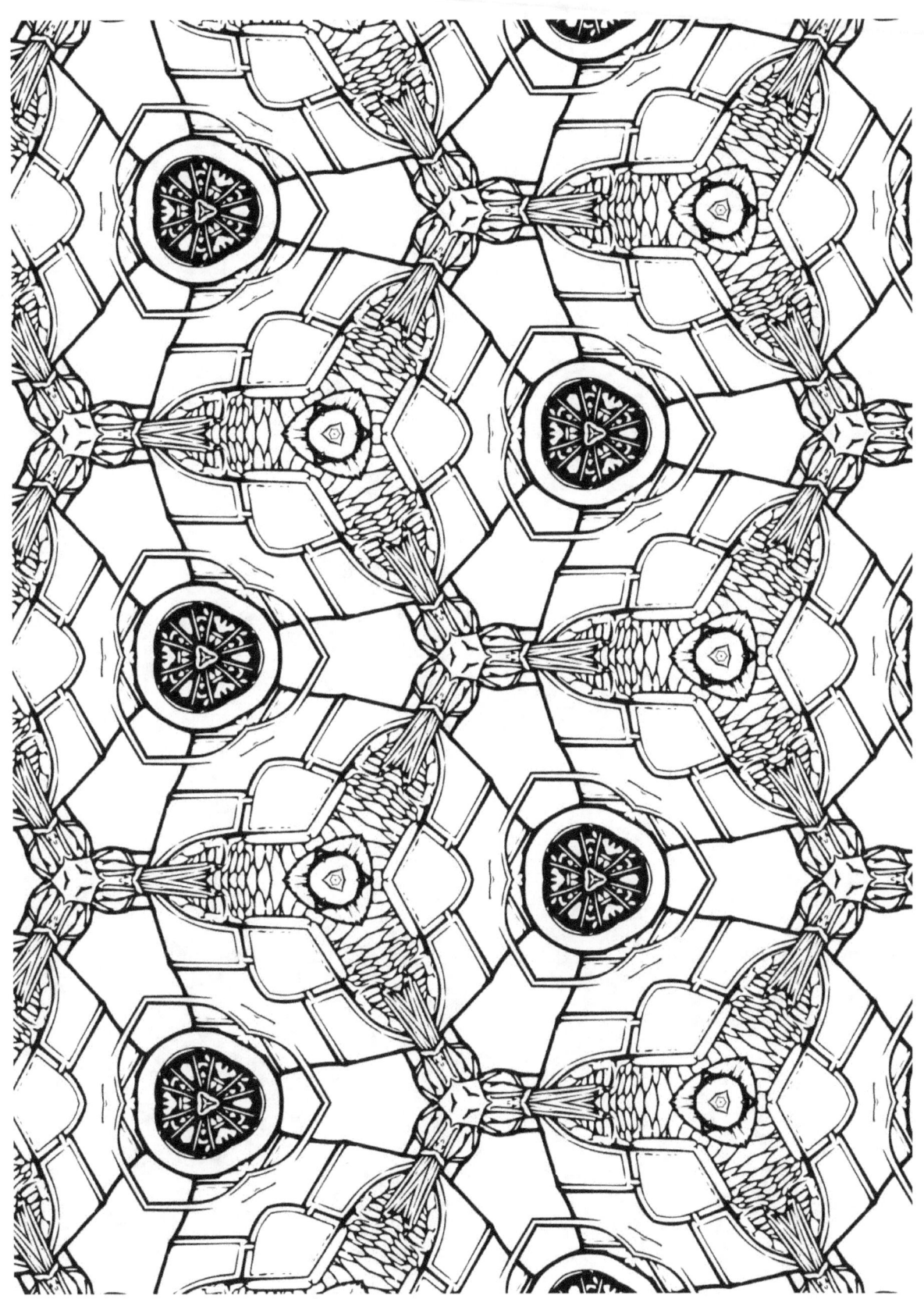

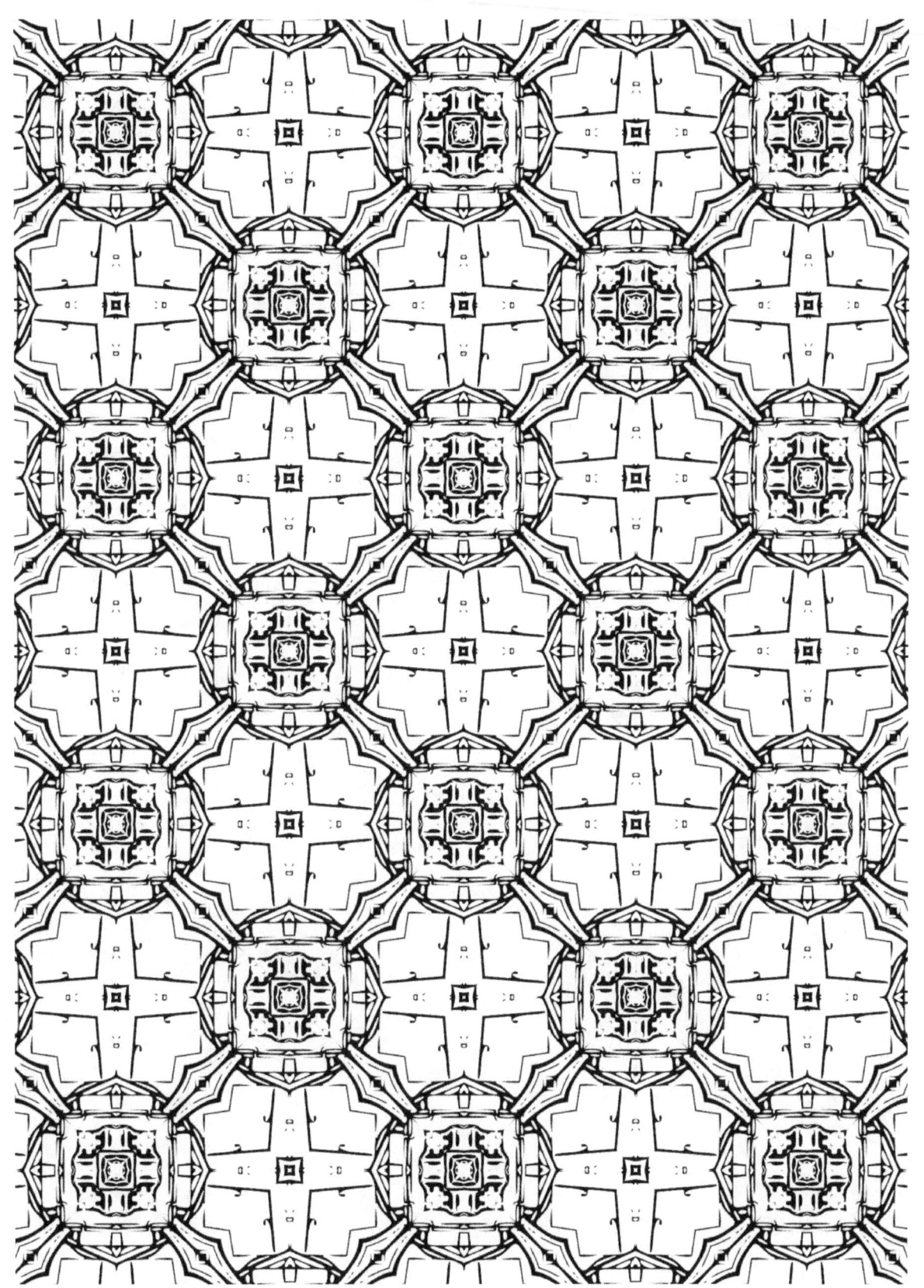

If you enjoyed this meditative adult coloring book, please visit Amazon.com and search for **"Better Than Zen Adult Coloring Book"** to discover our other books in this series.

You are also invited to visit AddictedToColoring.com for more books, tips and adult coloring fun.

www.ingramcontent.com/pod-product-compliance
Lightning Source LLC
Chambersburg PA
CBHW080551190526
45169CB00007B/2730